NEW ZEALAND

WORLD ADVENTURES

BY HARRIET BRUNDLE

BookLife

©2017
Book Life
King's Lynn
Norfolk PE30 4LS

ISBN: 978-1-78637-139-3

Written by:
Harriet Brundle

Edited by:
Charlie Ogden

Designed by:
Danielle Jones

A catalogue record for this book
is available from the British Library.

NEW ZEALAND
WORLD ADVENTURES

CONTENTS

Words in **red** can be found in the glossary on page 24.

WHERE IS NEW ZEALAND?

New Zealand is made up of two large islands, called the North Island and South Island. There are also many smaller islands.

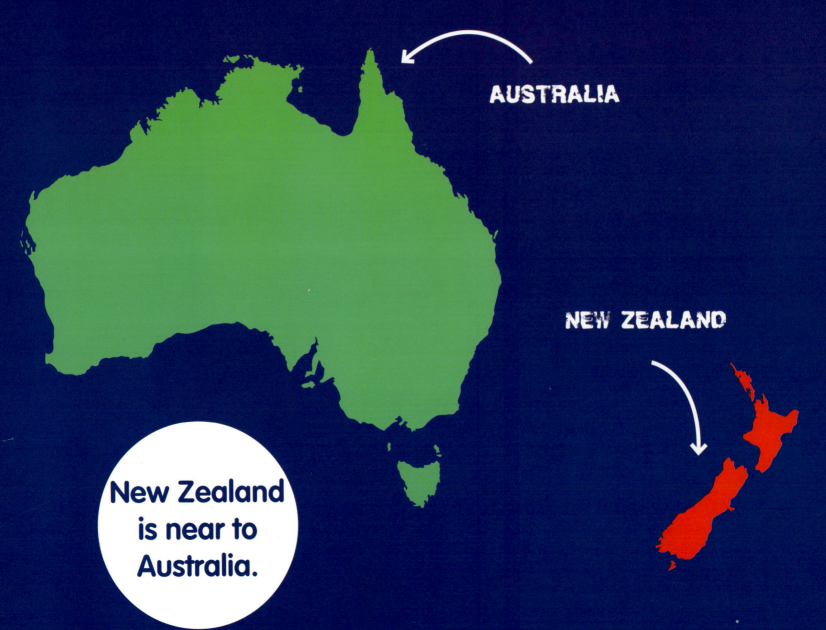

AUSTRALIA

NEW ZEALAND

New Zealand is near to Australia.

This is the flag of New Zealand.

The biggest city in New Zealand is called Auckland. Over four million people live in New Zealand.

WEATHER AND LANDSCAPE

The weather in New Zealand is usually warm and sunny. The warmest months in New Zealand are December, January and February.

There are many mountains in New Zealand.
The highest mountain in New Zealand is called
Mount Cook.

Mount Cook

PEOPLE IN NEW ZEALAND

The Māori name for Mount Cook is Aoraki.

The **native** people of New Zealand are called the Māori. There are over half a million Māori people living in New Zealand today.

It is **traditional** for Māori people to have tattoos. Their tattoos tell people about their family and where they came from.

Traditional Māori tattoos are called Tā Moko.

CLOTHING

Many people in New Zealand wear **modern** clothes. When it is hot, people often wear t-shirts and shorts.

Today, many Māori people wear modern clothes.

Traditionally, Māori people made their clothes out of plants and animal skins. They also made necklaces and rings out of animal bones.

RELIGON

Over two million people in New Zealand follow Christianity. Lots of other people in New Zealand do not follow any **religion**.

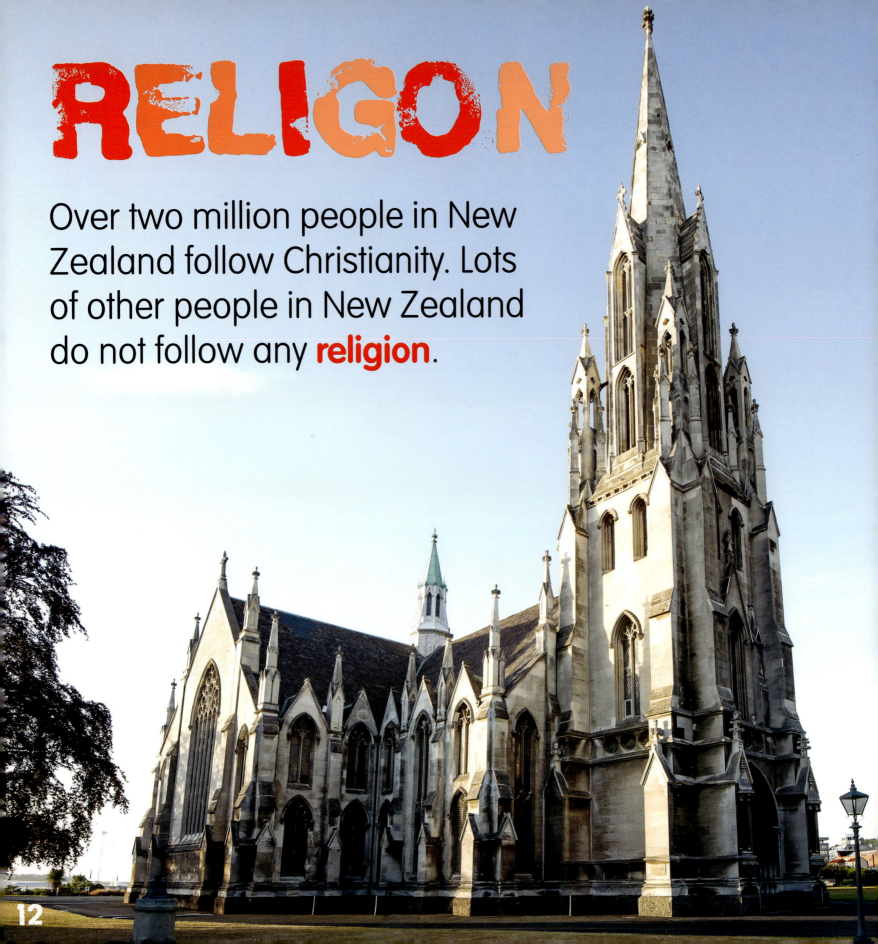

Māori people have their own set of beliefs, but many also follow Christianity.

FOOD

Fish is very **popular** in New Zealand. There are lots of places to catch fish around the islands.

Fish and chips are very popular in New Zealand.

Hāngī cooking is still used for special occasions.

Māori people used to cook meat using hot stones. This traditional way of cooking is called Hāngī.

AT SCHOOL

Children in New Zealand usually go to school from the age of six. Children learn about maths, science and English.

Some schools in New Zealand also teach the Māori language.

Many children use computers to help them study while they are at school.

FAMILIES

There are many different kinds of family in New Zealand. Some families are very big and some are very small.

Many Māori people believe that family is very important. Traditionally, Māori families would live together.

Knowing your family history is very important to Māori people.

SPORT

The most popular sport in New Zealand is rugby. New Zealand is known to have one of the best rugby teams in the world.

New Zealand's rugby team is called the All Blacks.

Another popular sport in New Zealand is netball. The New Zealand netball team is called the Silver Ferns.

FUN FACTS

For every one person in New Zealand there are nine sheep!

New Zealand is made up of over 30 islands.

New Zealand is the only country in the world where you can find kiwi birds.

Kiwi Bird

The Māori name for New Zealand is Aotearoa.

GLOSSARY

islands   areas of land that are surrounded by water

modern   something from present or recent times

native   people who were born in or come from a particular place

popular   liked by lots of people

religion   the belief in and worship of a god or gods

traditional   related to very old behaviours or beliefs

INDEX